The Greatest Pop Hits *of* 1996-1997

Project Manager: Carol Cuellar
Cover Design: Joseph Klucar

Contents

BECAUSE YOU LOVED ME
(Theme from "Up Close & Personal")

Words and Music by
DIANE WARREN
Arranged by DAN COATES

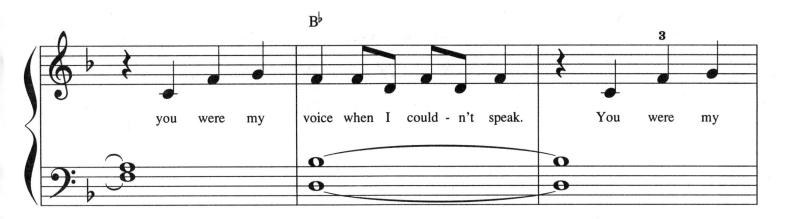

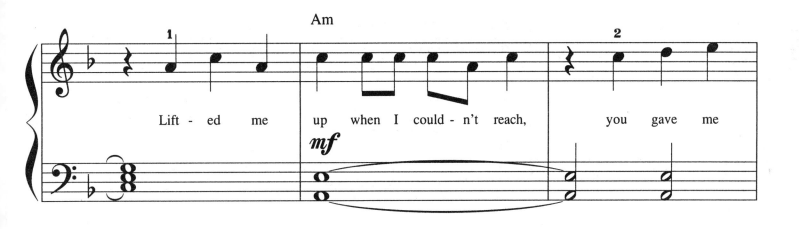

ALL OF MY LIFE

Arranged by
JOHN BRIMHALL

Lyrics by
ALAN and MARILYN BERGMAN
Music by
BARBRA STREISAND and MARVIN HAMLISCH

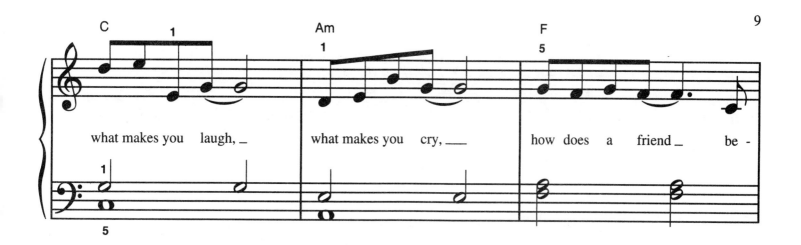

what makes you laugh, _ what makes you cry, ___ how does a friend _ be -

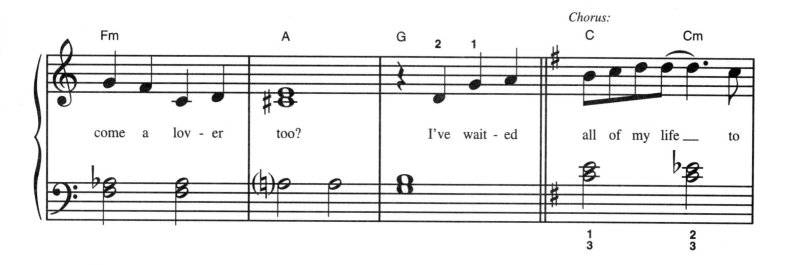

Chorus:

come a lov - er too? I've wait - ed all of my life _ to

find some-one who'd need my heart and read my mind, to light my

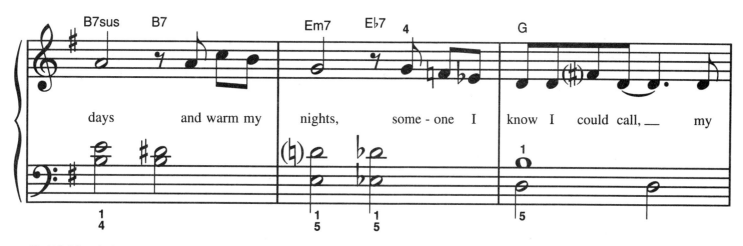

days and warm my nights, some - one I know I could call, _ my

ALWAYS BE MY BABY

Words and Music by
MANUEL SEAL, JERMAINE DUPRI
and MARIAH CAREY

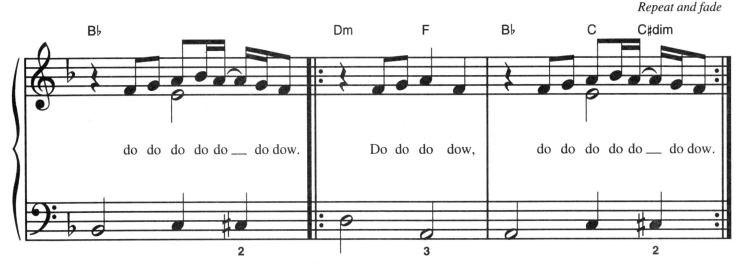

Verse 2:
I ain't gonna cry, no,
And I won't beg you to stay.
If you're determined to leave, boy,
I will not stand in your way.
But inevitably, you'll be back again,
'Cause you know in your heart, babe,
Our love will never end, no.

Verse 3:
We were as one, babe, for a moment in time.
And it seemed everlasting,
That you would always be mine.
Now you want to be free, so I'll let you fly.
'Cause you know in your heart, babe,
Our love will never end, no.

BE MY LOVER

Arranged by
JOHN BRIMHALL

Words and Music by
GERD AMIR SARAF, ANDY BRENNER,
MELANIE THORNTON and LANE McCRAY

Be My Lover - 5 - 1

BLESSED

Lyrics by
BERNIE TAUPIN

Music by
ELTON JOHN
Arranged by DAN COATES

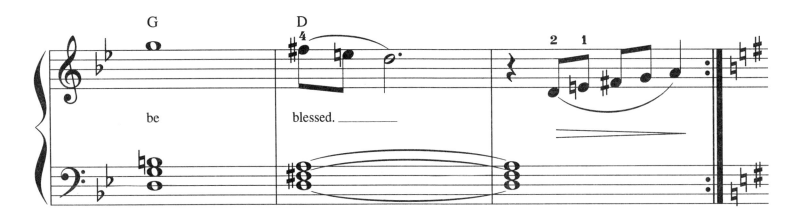

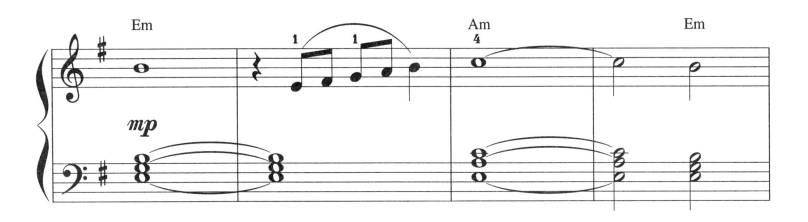

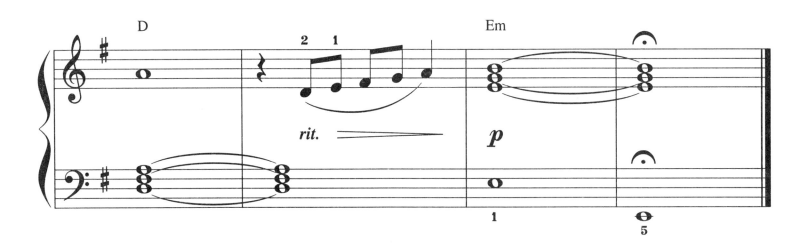

Verse 3:
I need you,
before I'm too old,
To have and to hold,
To walk with you
And watch you grow,
And know that you're blessed.

BREAKFAST AT TIFFANY'S

Words and Music by
TODD PIPES

Moderately ♩ = 104

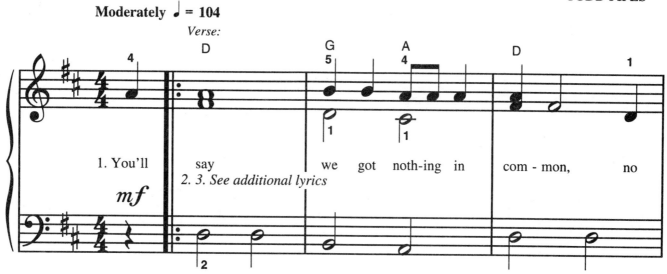

Breakfast at Tiffany's - 3 - 1

26

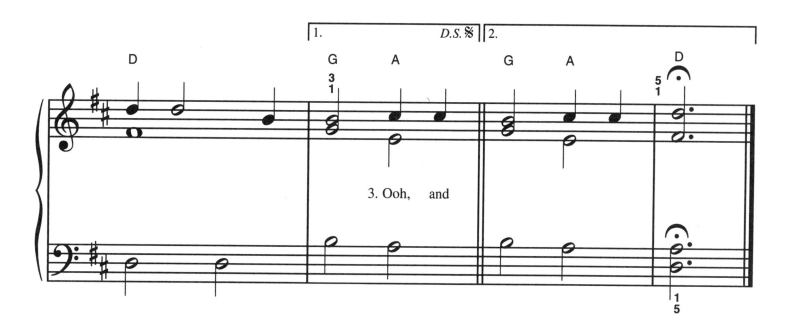

Verse 2:

I see you, the only one who knew me,
But now your eyes see through me.
I guess I was wrong. So what now?
It's plain to see we're over,
I hate when things are over,
When so much is left undone.

Verse 3:

You'll say we got nothing in common,
No common ground to start from,
And we're falling apart.
You'll say the world has come between us,
Our lives have come between us,
Still I know you just don't care.

BY HEART

Composed by
JIM BRICKMAN and
HOLLYE LEVEN
Arranged by DAN COATES

By Heart - 3 - 1

CHILDREN

Arranged by
JOHN BRIMHALL

Music by
ROBERTO CONCINO

Children - 3 - 1

32

CHANGE THE WORLD

Words and Music by
TOMMY SIMS, GORDON KENNEDY
and WAYNE KIRKPATRICK
Arranged by DAN COATES

Moderately slow

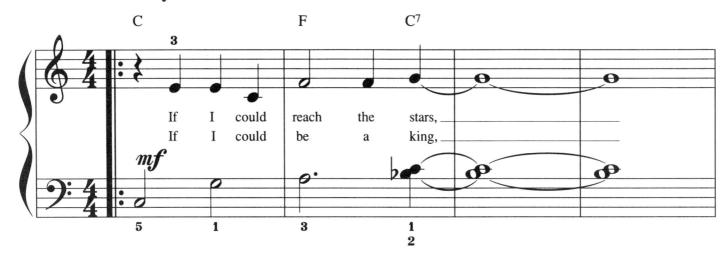

If I could reach the stars, _____
If I could be a king, _____

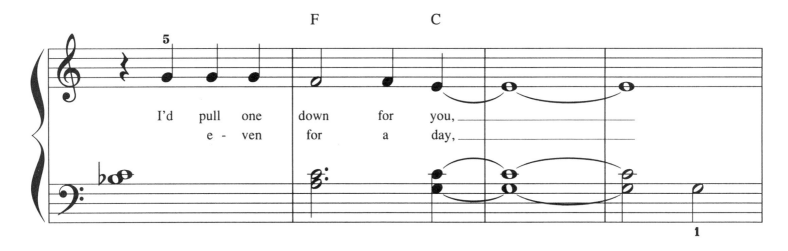

I'd pull one down for you, _____
e - ven for a day, _____

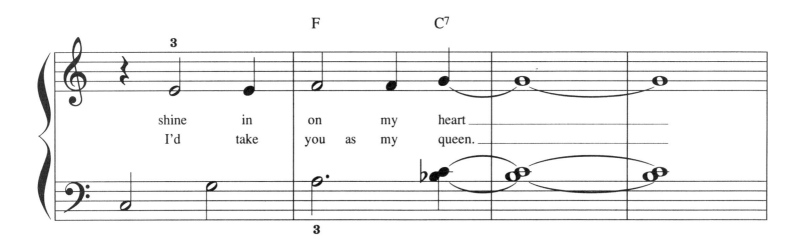

shine in on my heart _____
I'd take you as my queen. _____

so you could   see   the   truth,____
I'd have it   no oth - er   way.____

that   this   love   I   have   in - side____
And   our   love   would   rule____

is   ev - 'ry - thing   it   seems.____
in   this   king - dom   we   had   made.____

But   for   now,   I   find____
Till then I'll   be   a   fool,____

COUNT ON ME

Words and Music by
BABYFACE, WHITNEY HOUSTON
and **MICHAEL HOUSTON**
Arranged by DAN COATES

Count on me __ through thick and thin, a friend - ship that __ will nev - er end. When you are weak, __ I will be strong, help - ing you __ to car - ry on. __ Call on me, __ I will be there. Don't be a - fraid.

Count on Me - 3 - 1

FOLLOW YOU DOWN

Arranged by
JOHN BRIMHALL

Words and Music by
D. SCOTT JOHNSON, BILL LEEN, PHIL RHODES,
JESSE VALENZUELA and ROBIN WILSON

Follow You Down - 3 - 1

42

Verse 2:
I know we're headed somewhere, I can see how far we've come.
But still I can't remember anything.
Let's not do the wrong thing and I swear it might be fun.
It's a long way down when all the knots we've tied have come undone.
(To Chorus:)

Verse 3:
How you ever gonna find your place,
Running at an artificial pace?
Are they going to find us lying face down in the sand?
So, what the hell, now we've already been forever damned.
(To Chorus:)

DANCE INTO THE LIGHT

Arranged by
JOHN BRIMHALL

Words and Music by
PHIL COLLINS

Verse 2:
There'll be no more hiding in the shadows of fear.
There'll be no more chains to hold you.
The future is yours, you hold the key.
And there are no walls with freedom.

Bridge 2:
Now we're here, we won't go back.
We are one world, we have one voice.
Side by side, we are not afraid,
Because the train is coming to carry you home.
Come dance with me.
(To Chorus:)

Verse 3:
Do you see the sun? Yeah, it's a brand new day.
All of the world's in your hands, now use it.
What's past is past. Don't turn around.
Brush away the cobwebs of freedom.

Bridge 2:
Now we're here, there's no turning back.
You have each other, you have one voice.
Hand in hand, you can lay the tracks,
Because the train is coming to carry you home.
Come dance with me.
(To Chorus:)

(I Wanna Take) FOREVER TONIGHT

Arranged by
JOHN BRIMHALL

Words and Music by
ANDY GOLDMARK and
ERIC CARMEN

Verse 2:
Touch my lips, I'm on fire.
You're the only one I'll ever desire.
Turn the lights down low, let the world go slow.
When I'm holding you tonight, it's so easy.
Nothing moves me like you do when you tease me.
And to rush would be a crime,
I just wanna spend some time with you, baby.

(I Wanna Take) Forever Tonight - 4 - 4

HERO'S DREAM

Composed by
JIM BRICKMAN
Arranged by DAN COATES

Moderately, with spirit

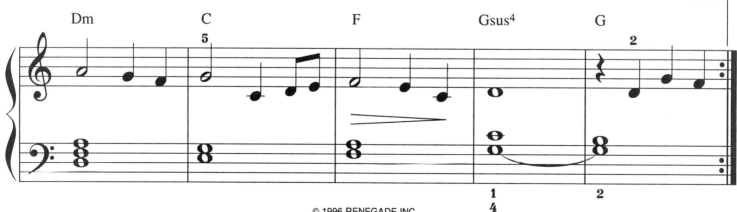

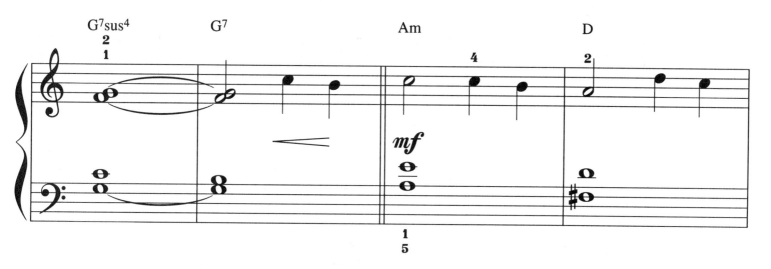

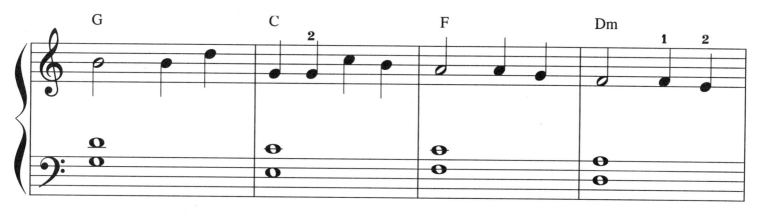

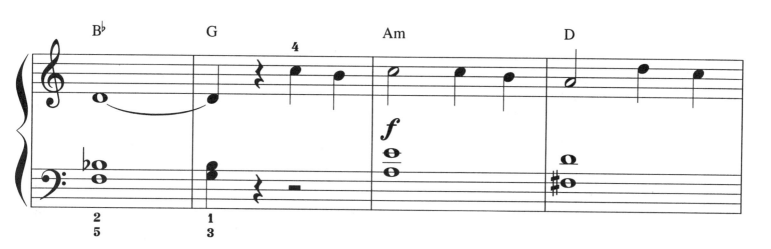

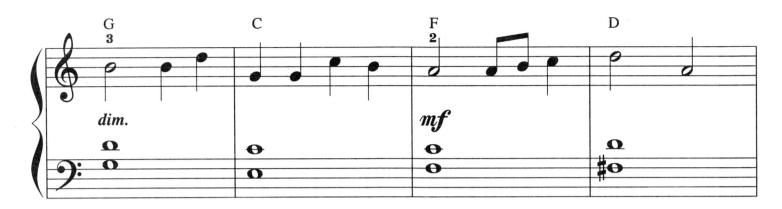

D.C. al Coda

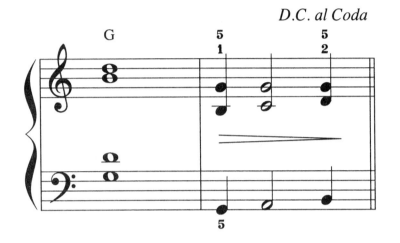

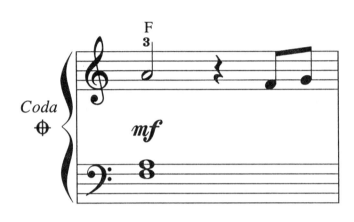

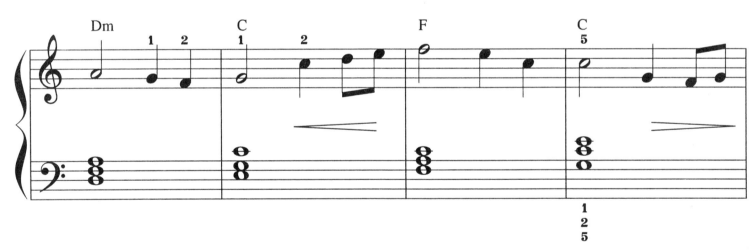

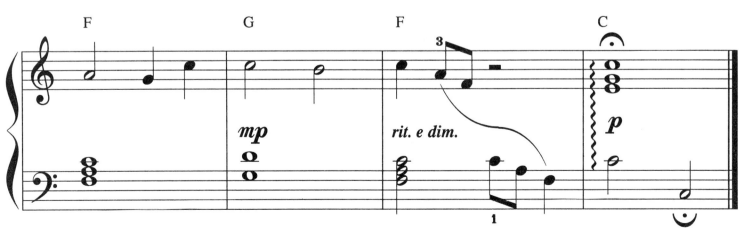

From the Motion Picture "THE PREACHER'S WIFE"

I BELIEVE IN YOU AND ME

Words and Music by
SANDY LINZER and DAVID WOLFERT
Arranged by DAN COATES

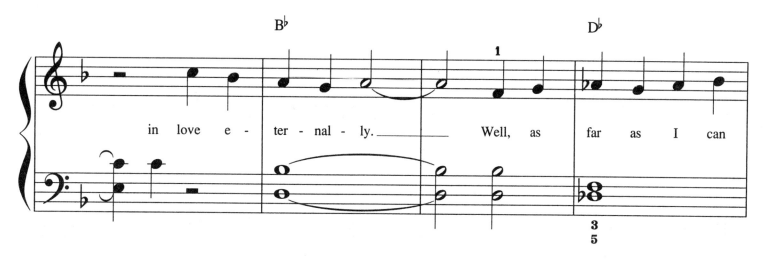

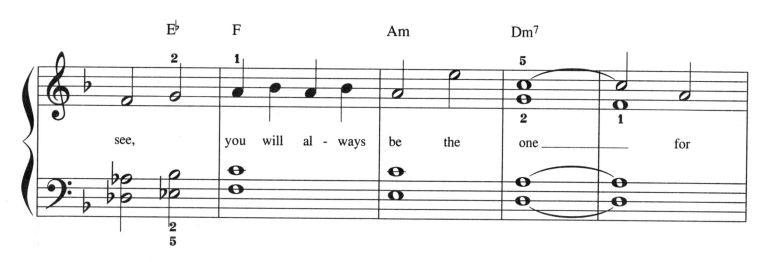

I Believe in You and Me - 5 - 1

54

56

lost, _____ now I'm free, _____ 'cause

I be - lieve in you and me.

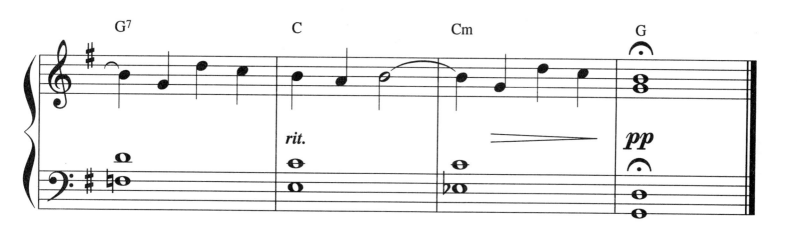

Verse 2:
I will never leave you side,
I will never hurt your pride.
When all the chips are down,
I will always be around
Just to be right where you are, my love.
Oh, I love you, boy.
I will never leave you out,
I will always let you in
To places no one has ever been.
Deep inside, can't you see?
I believe in you and me.

I BELIEVE I CAN FLY

Words and Music by
R. KELLY
Arranged by DAN COATES

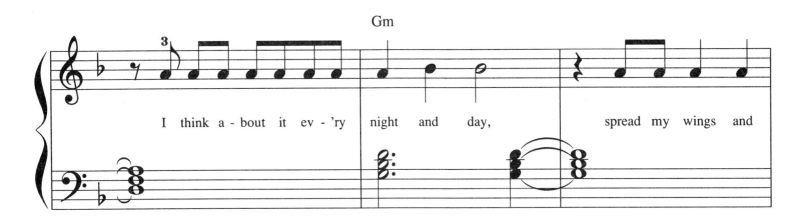

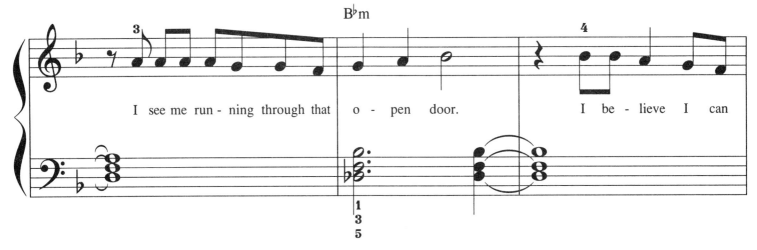

From the Motion Picture "THE MIRROR HAS TWO FACES"

I FINALLY FOUND SOMEONE

Words and Music by
BARBRA STREISAND, MARVIN HAMLISCH,
R.J. LANGE and BRYAN ADAMS
Arranged by DAN COATES

Moderately slow

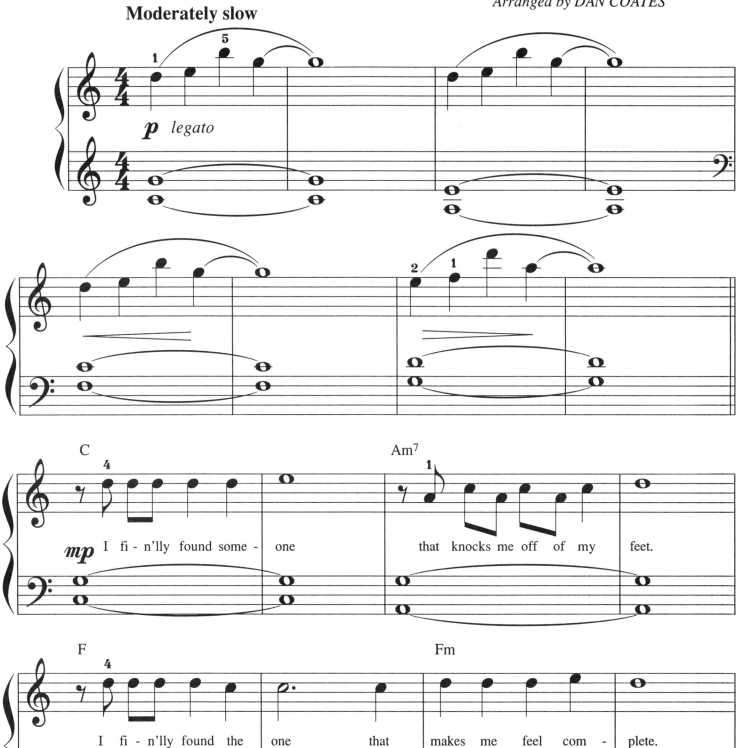

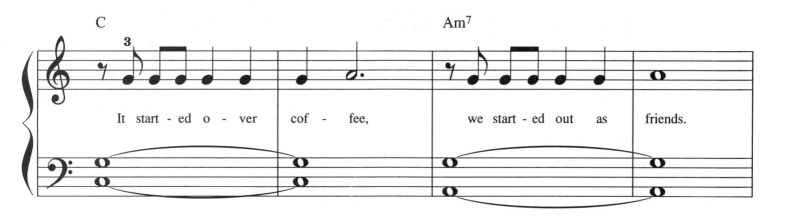

It start - ed o - ver cof - fee, we start - ed out as friends.

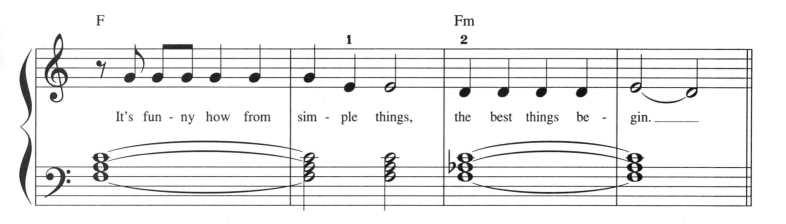

It's fun - ny how from sim - ple things, the best things be - gin. ____

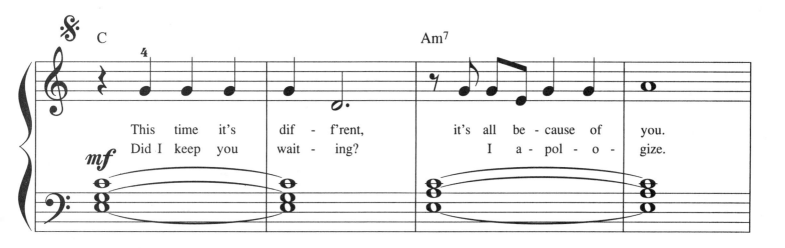

This time it's dif - f'rent, it's all be - cause of you.
Did I keep you wait - ing? I a - pol - o - gize.

It's bet - ter than it's ev - er been 'cause we can talk it through. ____
I will wait for - ev - er just to know you were mine. ____

I Finally Found Someone - 5 - 2

64

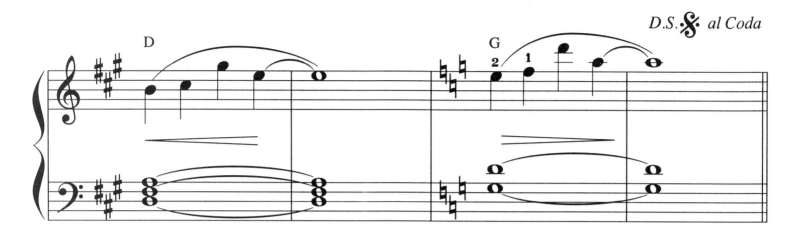

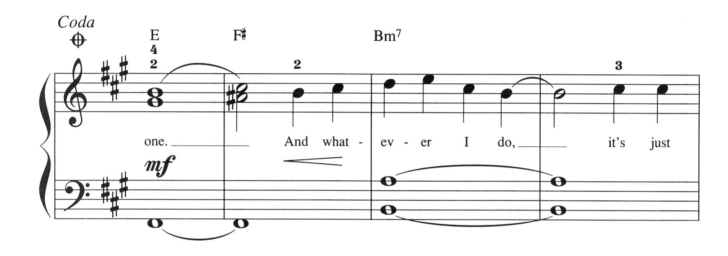

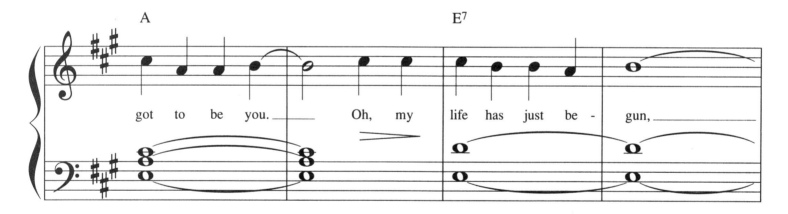

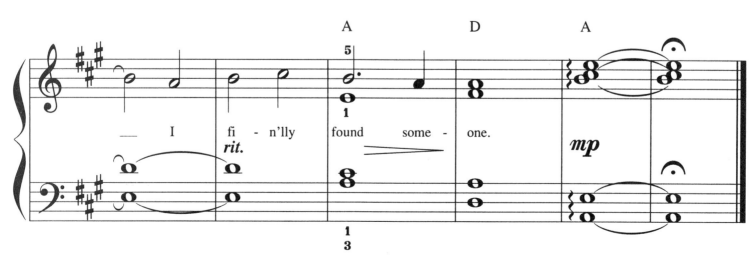

IF IT MAKES YOU HAPPY

Arranged by
JOHN BRIMHALL

Words and Music by
SHERYL CROW and JEFF TROTT

Moderately slow ♩ = 96

1. I've been long, a long way from
2.3. *See additional lyrics*

here. Put on a pon - cho,

played for mos - qui - tos, and drank 'til I was thirst - y a - gain. We went

search - ing through thrift store jun - gles, found Ge -

If It Makes You Happy - 3 - 1

68

69

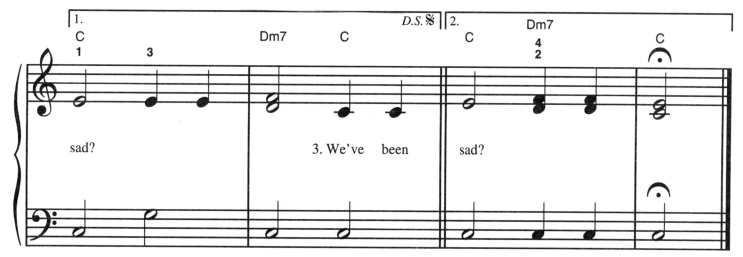

Verse 2:
You get down, real low down.
You listen to Coltrane,
Derail your own train.
Well, who hasn't been there before?
I come 'round, around the hard way.
Bring your comics in bed,
Scrape the mold off the bread,
And serve you French toast again.
Well, O.K., I still get stoned.
I'm not the kind of girl you'd take home.

Chorus:
If it makes you happy,
It can't be that bad.
If it makes you happy,
Then why the hell are you so sad?

Verse 3:
We've been far, far away from here.
Put on a poncho, played for mosquitos,
And everywhere in between.
Well, O.K., we get along.
So what if right now everything's wrong?

If It Makes You Happy - 3 - 3

I LOVE YOU ALWAYS FOREVER

Words and Music by
DONNA LEWIS
Arranged by DAN COATES

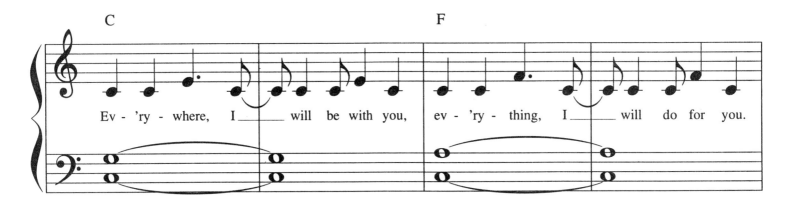

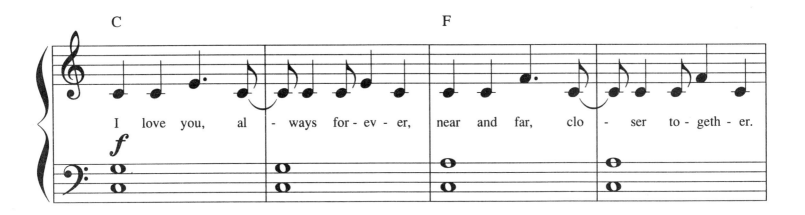

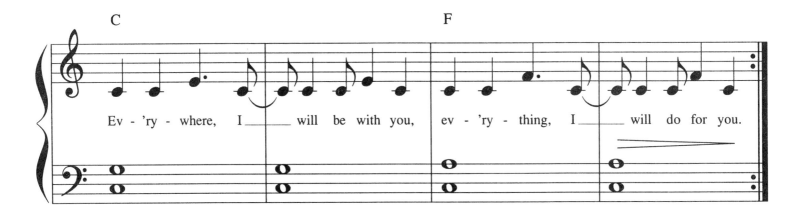

I Love You Always Forever - 4 - 3

Verse 2:
Thoses days of warm rain come rushing back to me,
Miles of windless, summer night air.
Secret moments shared in the heat of the afternoon,
Out of the stillness, soft spoken words. *(Chorus:)*

Verse 3:
You've got the most unbelievable blue eyes I've ever seen.
You've got me almost melting away as we lay there
Under blue sky with pure white stars,
Exotic sweetness, a magical time. *(Chorus:)*

I WANT TO COME OVER

Arranged by
JOHN BRIMHALL

Words and Music by
MELISSA ETHERIDGE

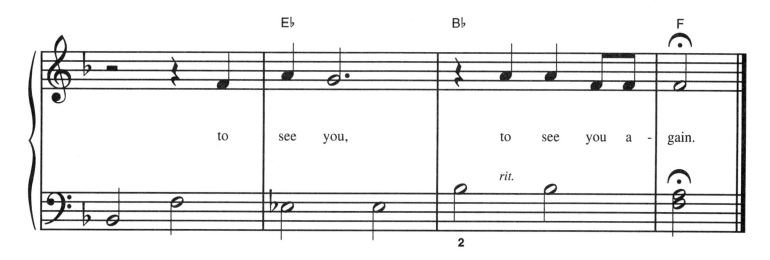

Verse 2:
I know your friend, you told her about me.
She filled you with fear, some kind of sin.
How can you turn, denying the fire?
Lover, I burn, let me in.
(To Bridge:)

Verse 3:
I know you're confused, I know that you're shaken.
You think we'll be lost, once we begin.
I know that you're weak, I know that you want me.
Lover, don't speak, let me in.
(To Bridge:)

I'M NOT GIVING YOU UP

Arranged by
JOHN BRIMHALL

Words by
GLORIA ESTEFAN
Music by
KIKE SANTANDER

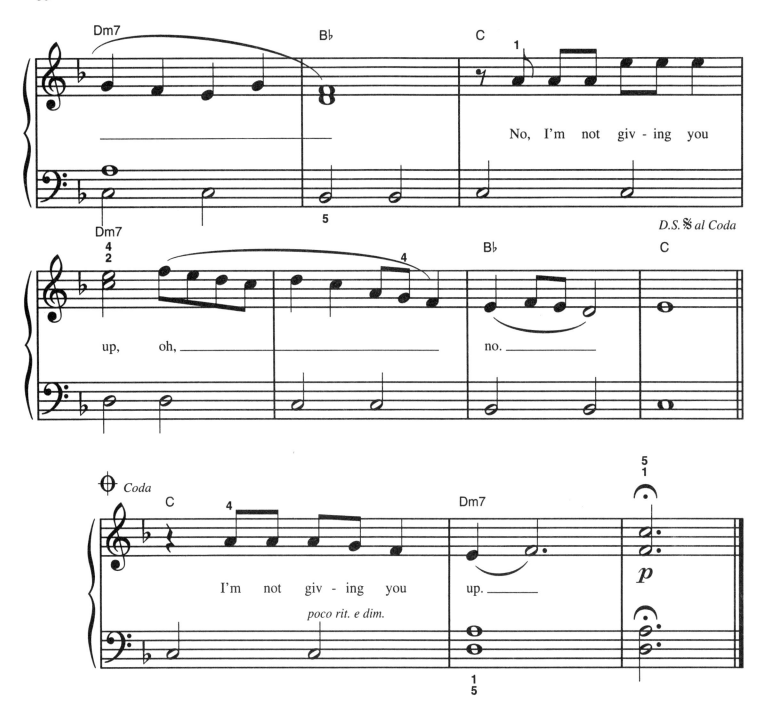

Verse 2:
Thinking back, I see what we have is something different.
I think we've known all along.
So how fair would it be to divide this love's existence
Between what's right and what's wrong.
And you, always wond'ring if we'll make it.
Time will tell you that I'm not giving you up.
Oh, no, no, no.
(To Bridge:)

Verse 3:
Screaming in the silence, the promises we've spoken
Come back to haunt me, false and broken.
Quiet desperation to see we're lost forever,
Searching for water in this desert.
No, I refuse to have to do without your kisses.
I'm not giving you up, no, no.
(To Bridge:)

KILLING ME SOFTLY
(WITH HIS SONG)

Words by
NORMAN GIMBLE

Music by
CHARLES FOX
Arranged by DAN COATES

82

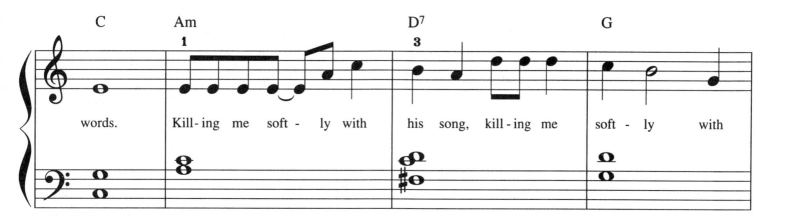

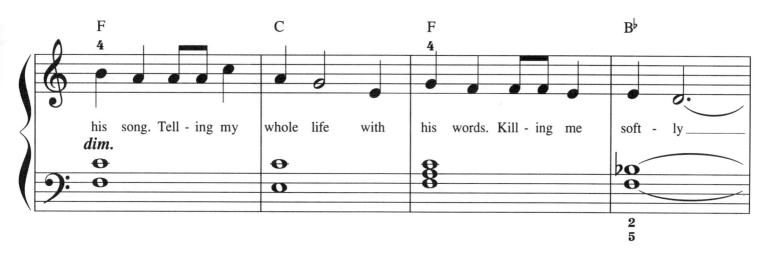

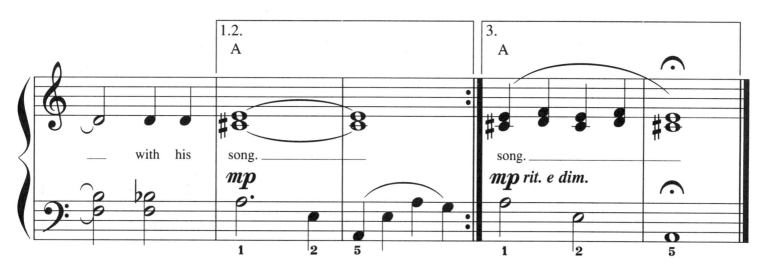

Verse 3:
He sang as if he knew me,
In all my dark despair.
And then he looked right through me
As if I wasn't there.
But he was there, this stranger
Singing clear and strong.
(To Chorus:)

KEY WEST INTERMEZZO
(I SAW YOU FIRST)

Arranged by
JOHN BRIMHALL

Words and Music by
JOHN MELLENCAMP
and GEORGE GREEN

No one wants to be lone-ly, no one wants to sing the blues.

Verses 2, 3 & 4:

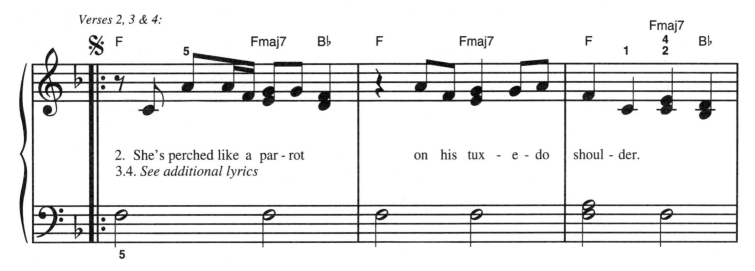

2. She's perched like a par - rot on his tux - e - do shoul - der.
3.4. *See additional lyrics*

Christ, what's she doin' with him? She could be danc-ing with me.

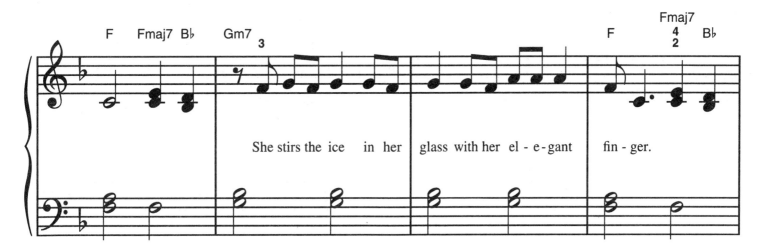

She stirs the ice in her glass with her el - e - gant fin - ger.

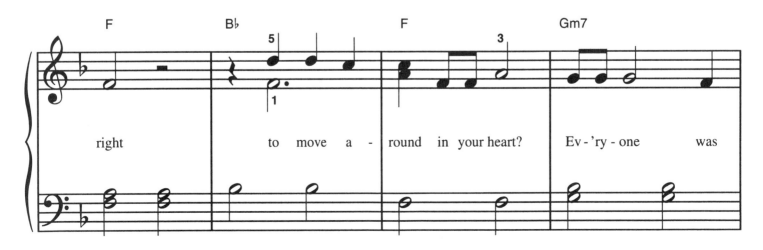

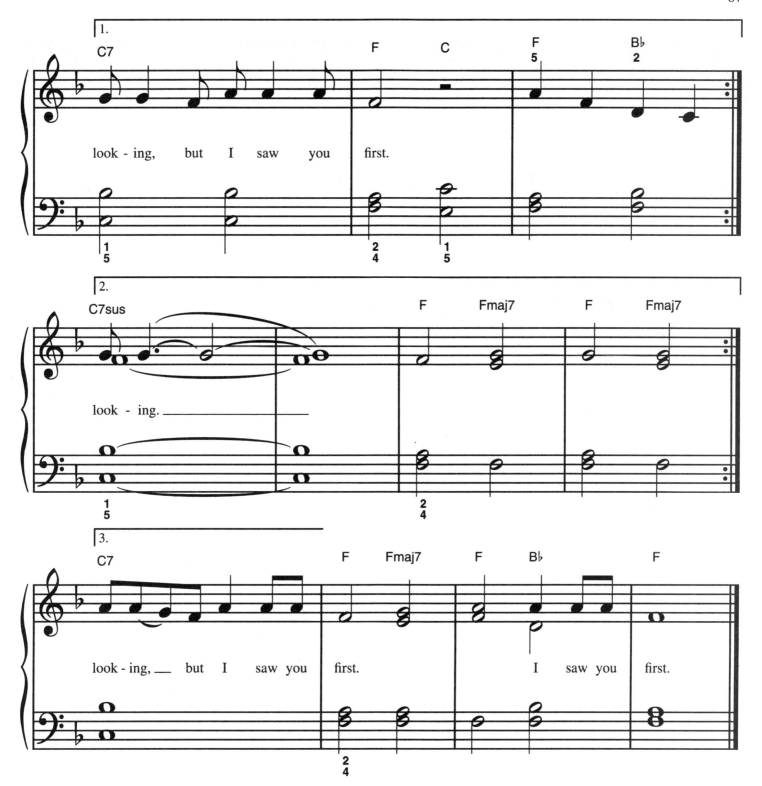

Verse 3:
On a moon spattered road in her parrot rebozo,
Gypsy Scotty is driving his big, long, yellow car.
She flies like a bird over his shoulder.
She whispers in his ear, "Boy, you are my star."
(To Chorus:)

Verse 4:
In the bone colored dawn, me and Gypsy Scotty are singin',
The radio is playing, she left her shoes out in the back.
He tells me a story about some girl he knows in Kentucky.
He just made that story up, there ain't no girl like that.
(To Chorus:)

LET'S MAKE A NIGHT TO REMEMBER

Arranged by
JOHN BRIMHALL

Words and Music by
BRYAN ADAMS and
ROBERT JOHN "MUTT" LANGE

Let's Make a Night to Remember - 5 - 1

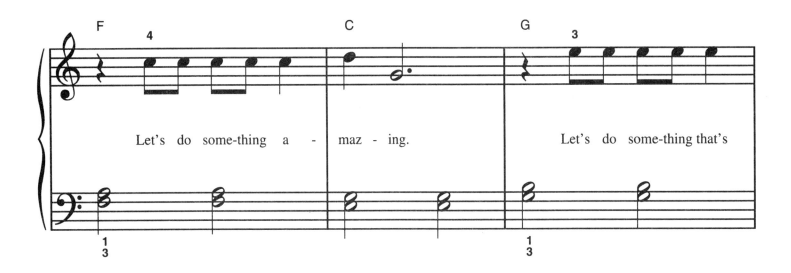

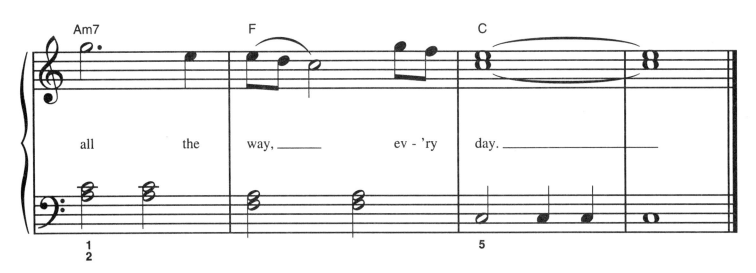

Verse 2:
I love the way ya move tonight,
Beads of sweat drippin' down your skin.
My lyin' here 'n' you lyin' there.
Our shadows on the wall and our hands everywhere.

LOVE IS THE POWER

Arranged by
JOHN BRIMHALL

Words and Music by
MICHAEL BOLTON, DIANE WARREN
and WALTER AFANASIEFF

Love Is the Power - 3 - 1

94

Love Is the Power - 3 - 2

MACARENA

Arranged by
JOHN BRIMHALL

Words and Music by
ANTONIO ROMERO and RAFAEL RUIZ

Macarena - 3 - 1

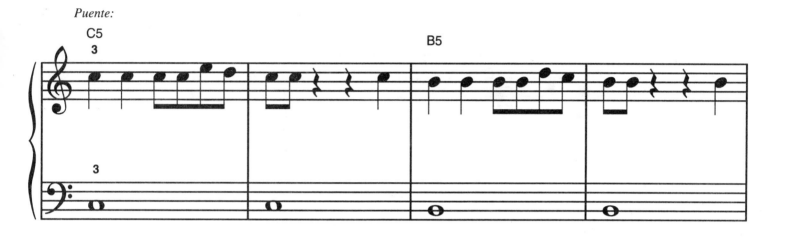

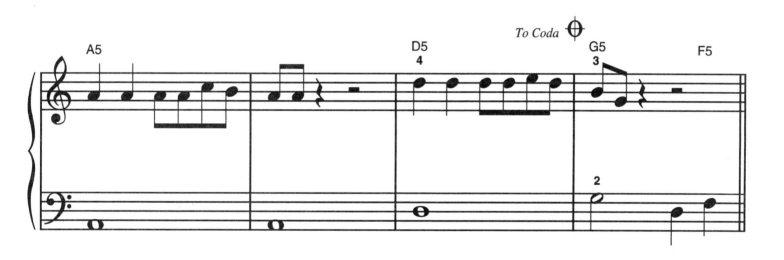

Macarena - 3 - 2

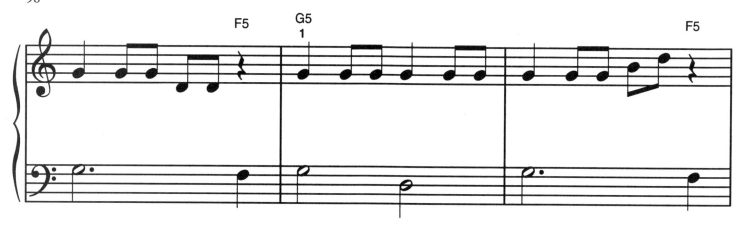

Coro:
Dale a tu cuerpo alegría Macarena
Que tu cuerpo es pa' darle alegría y cosa buena.
Dale a tu cuerpo alegría Macarena, eh, Macarena.

Dale a tu cuerpo alegría Macarena
Que tu cuerpo es pa' darle alegría y cosa buena.
Dale a tu cuerpo alegría Macarena, eh, Macarena.

Verso 1:
Macarena tiene un novio que se llama,
Que se llama de apellido Vitorino.
Y en la jura de bandera del muchacho
Se la dió con dos amigos.

Puente 1:
Macarena tiene un novio que se llama,
Que se llama de apellido Vitorino.
Y en la jura de bandera del muchacho
Se la dió con dos amigos.
(Al Coro:)

Verso 2:
Macarena, Macarena, Macarena,
Que te gustan los veranos de Marbelia.
Macarena, Macarena, Macarena,
Que te gusto la movida guerrillera.
(Al Coro:)

Verso 3:
Macarena sueña con el Corte inglés
Y se compra los modelos mas modernos.
Le gustaría vivir en Nueva York
Y ligar un novio nuevo.

Puente 2:
Macarena sueña con el Corte inglés
Y se compra los modelos mas modernos.
Le gustaría vivir en Nueva York
Y ligar un novio nuevo.
(Al Coro:)

Verso 4:
Macarena tiene un novio que se llama,
Que se llama de apellido Vitorino.
Y en la jura de bandera del muchacho
Se la dió con dos amigos.

Puente 3:
Macarena tiene un novio que se llama,
Que se llama de apellido Vitorino.
Y en la jura de bandera del muchacho
Se la dió con dos amigos.
(Al Coro:)

NOWHERE TO GO

Arranged by
JOHN BRIMHALL

Words and Music by
MELISSA ETHERIDGE

Moderately slow ♩ = 96
Verse:

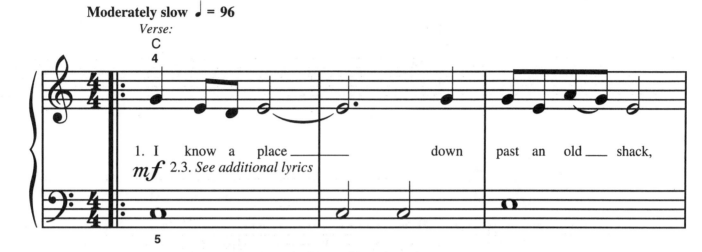

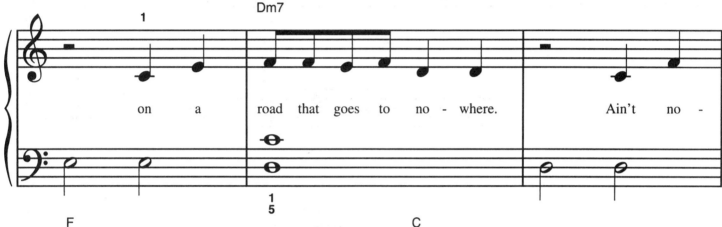

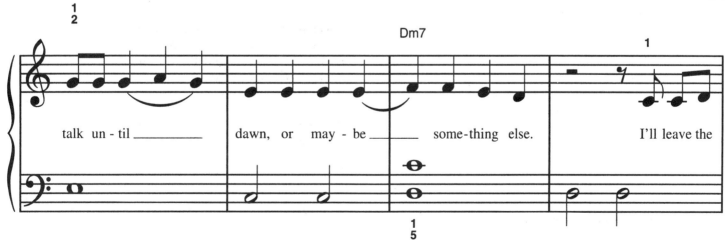

Nowhere to Go - 3 - 1

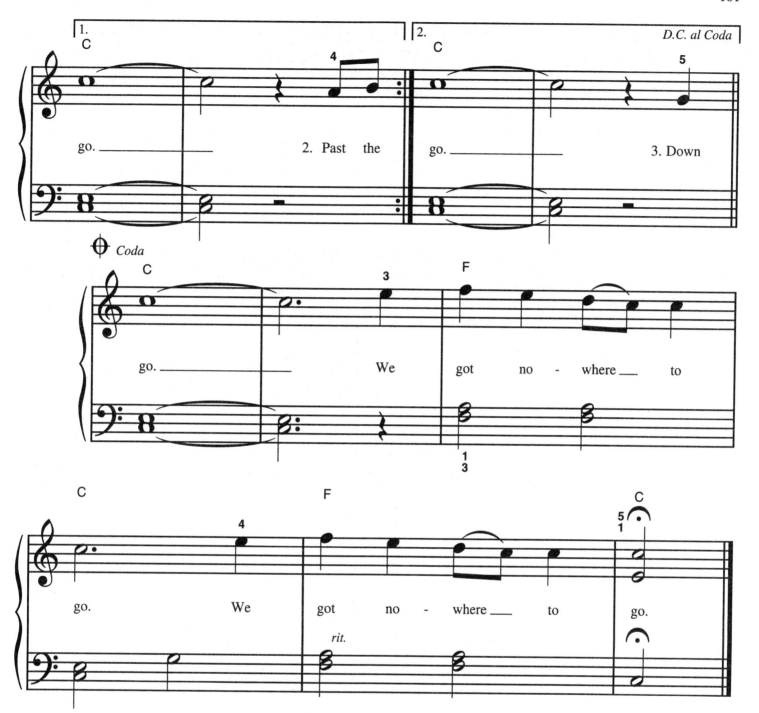

Verse 2:
Past the Walmart and the prison, down by the old V.A.
Just my jeans and my T shirt, and my blue Chevrolet.
It's Saturday night, feels like everything's wrong.
I've got some strawberry wine,
I want to get you alone, get you alone.

Verse 3:
Down by the muddy water of the mighty Mo,
In an old, abandoned boxcar, will I ever know?
Dance with me forever, this moment is divine.
I'm so close to heaven,
This hell is not mine, this hell is not mine.

ONE OF US

Words and Music by
ERIC BAZILIAN
Arranged by DAN COATES

1. If God had a name, ___
God had a face, ___

what would it be and would you call it to his face, if you were faced with him in
what would it look like and would you want to see, if see - ing meant that you would

all his glo - ry? What would you ask if you had just one ques - tion?
have to be - lieve in things like heav - en and in Je - sus and the saints and

One of Us - 3 - 2

UN-BREAK MY HEART

Words and Music by
DIANE WARREN
Arranged by DAN COATES

Moderately slow

106

Un-Break My Heart - 3 - 2

THE ONLY THING THAT LOOKS GOOD
ON ME IS YOU

Arranged by
JOHN BRIMHALL

Words and Music by
BRYAN ADAMS and
ROBERT JOHN "MUTT" LANGE

1. Well, I / don't look good in no Ar - ma - ni suits, no
sat - is - fied ___ with Ver - sa - ce style. Put those

Gu - cci shoes ___ or de - sign - er boots. I've / tried the lat - est lines ___ from
pat - ent lea - ther pants in the cir - cu - lar file. / Some - times I think I might be

A to Z, but there's / just one thing that looks / good on me.
look - in' good, but there's / on - ly one thing that fits me / like it should.

Chorus:

The on - ly thing I / want, / the on - ly thing I

The Only Thing That Looks Good on Me Is You - 4 - 1

The Only Thing That Looks Good on Me Is You - 4 - 2

110

The Only Thing That Looks Good on Me Is You - 4 - 3

The Only Thing That Looks Good on Me Is You - 4 - 4

REACH

Words and Music by
GLORIA ESTEFAN and
DIANE WARREN
Arranged by RICHARD BRADLEY

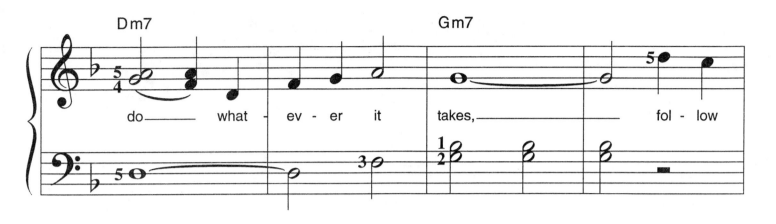

do ___ what - ev - er it takes, ___ fol - low

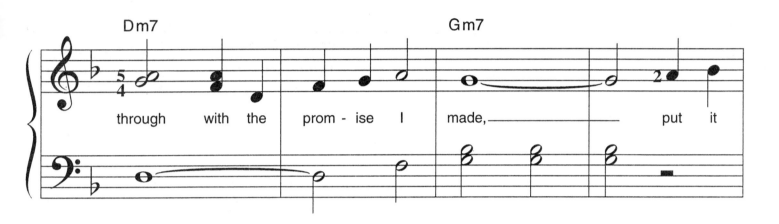

through with the prom - ise I made, ___ put it

all on the line, ___ what I hope for at last ___ would be

mine ___ if I could reach ___

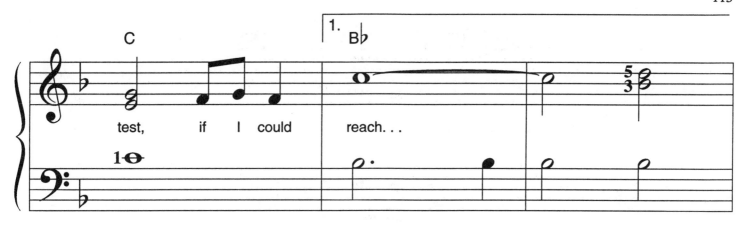

test,   if   I   could   reach. . .

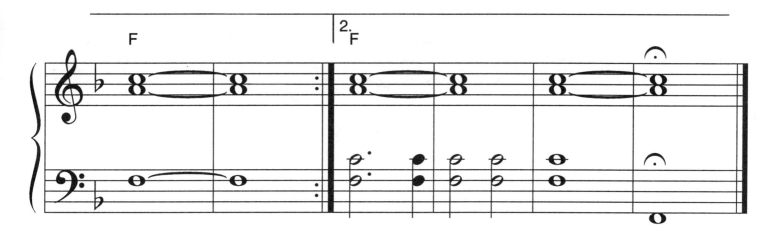

Verse 2:
Some days are meant to be remembered.
Those days we rise above the stars.
So, I'll go the distance this time,
Seeing more the higher I climb
That the more I believe,
All the more that this dream will be mine.

SEND ME A LOVER

Arranged by
JOHN BRIMHALL

Words and Music by
RICHARD HAHN and
GEORGE THATCHER

Moderately slow ♩ = 80

Verse:

1. I was-n't search-ing to end this hurt-ing,
2. *See additional lyrics*

but out of no - where you made me ___ feel. ___

I cried a - bout it, I lied a - bout it,

and tried to doubt this could be real. ___

118

Verse 2:
It still astounds me, the way you found me,
It's almost too good to be true.
From our first meeting, I had the feeling
The rest of my life I'd spend with you.
I just can't turn my back on what I know is true.
I'm into you in every way.

THAT THING YOU DO!

Words and Music by
ADAM SCHLESINGER
Arranged by DAN COATES

Bright rock tempo

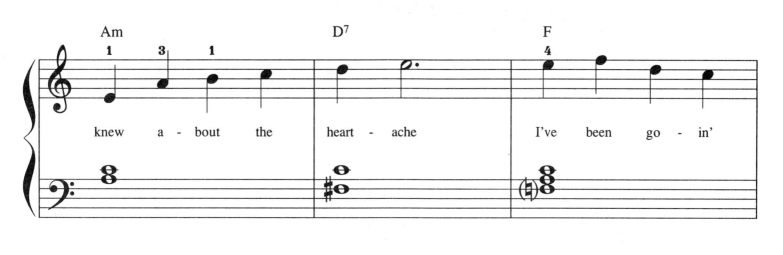

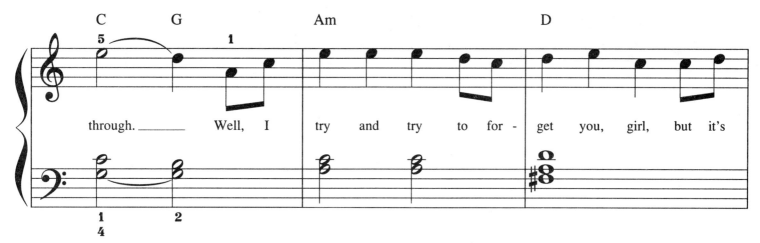

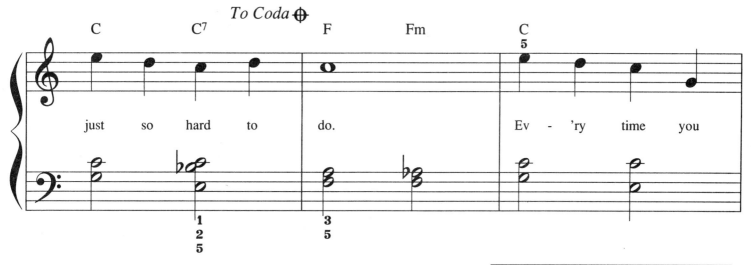

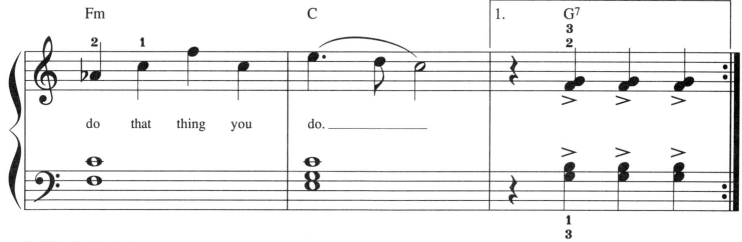

123

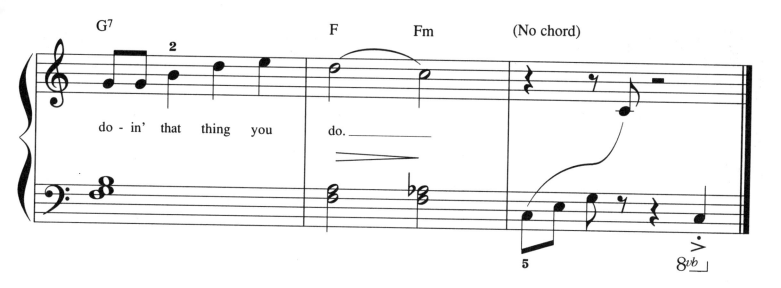

Verse 2:
I know all the games you play.
And I'm gonna find a way to let you know
That you'll be mine someday.
'Cause we could be happy, can't you see?
If you'd only let me be the one to hold you
And keep you here with me.
'Cause I try and try to forget you, girl,
But it's just too hard to do.
Every time you do that thing you do.

Verse 3:
(8 Bar Instrumental Solo...)
'Cause we could be happy, can't you see?
If you'd only let me be the one to hold you
And keep you here with me.
'Cause it hurts me so just to see you go
Around with someone new.
(To Coda:)

WHO WILL SAVE YOUR SOUL

Arranged by
JOHN BRIMHALL

Words and Music by
JEWEL KILCHER

Moderate shuffle ♩ = 112

Verse:

1. Peo - ple liv - in' their lives for you ___ on T ___ V, they say they're

bet - ter than you and you a - gree. ___

She says, "Hold ___ my calls," from be - hind those cold, ___ brick walls. She says

"Come here, boy, ___ there ain't ___ noth - in' for free."

128

YOU'LL BE MINE
(Party Time)

Arranged by
JOHN BRIMHALL

Words and Music by
EMILIO ESTEFAN, JR.,
LAWRENCE DERMER and CLAY OSTWALD

130

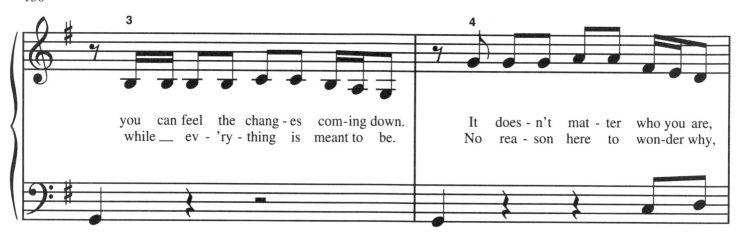

YOU'LL SEE

Arranged by
JOHN BRIMHALL

Words and Music by
MADONNA CICCONE and
DAVID FOSTER

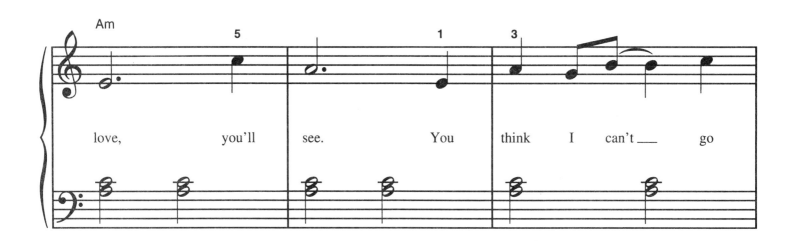

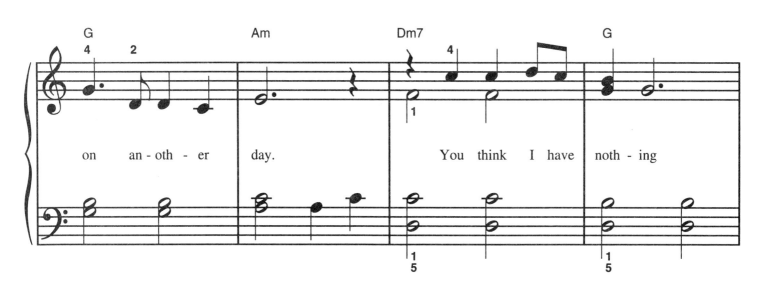

You'll See - 4 - 1

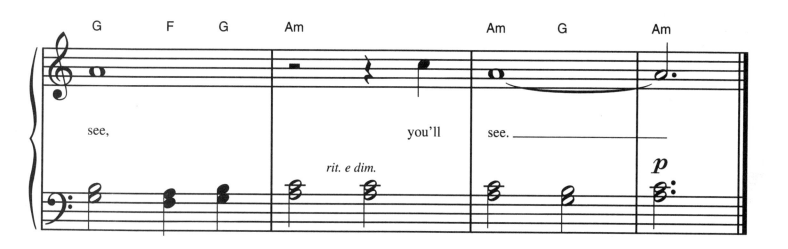

Verse 2:
You think that I can never laugh again, you'll see.
You think that you've destroyed my faith in love.
You think after all you've done,
I'll never find my way back home.
You'll see, somehow, someday.

Verse 3:
You think that you are strong,
But you are weak, you'll see.
It takes more strength to cry, admit defeat.
I have truth on my side, you only have deceit.
You'll see, somehow, someday.